BREAKING THE CYCLE OF DEBT:
Strategies for Reducing Financial Burdens and Increasing Wealth

NOAH JACKSON

Disclaimer

The information and resources provided in this book are for general purposes only and should not be considered as professional or expert advice. The author and publisher cannot be held responsible for any direct, indirect, incidental, or consequential damages resulting from the use of this book. The reader is solely responsible for their own actions and should always seek appropriate professional advice before making any decision based on the content of this book. The author and publisher make no claims or warranties about the completeness, accuracy, reliability, suitability, or availability of the information contained in this book. All views expressed are solely those of the author and do not necessarily reflect the views and opinions of the publisher. The reader bears the responsibility for their own financial decisions and the author and publisher shall not be held liable for any consequences resulting from their actions. Reading and implementing the strategies in this book are at the reader's own risk. The reader understands and agrees to these terms by accessing and reading this book.. Thank you for purchasing this book and we hope you find the information within helpful.

Table of Contents

Introduction: The Trap of Debt and the Journey to Financial Freedom

I have spent years researching and analyzing the various factors that contribute to the widespread issue of debt in our society. In this book, I hope to shed light on the traps that keep us in a cycle of debt and provide a roadmap for readers to break free and achieve financial empowerment. Through personal anecdotes, expert insights, and practical strategies, I aim to guide readers towards a path of financial stability and independence. Whether you are struggling with debt yourself or simply looking to improve your financial well-being, this book offers valuable insights and actionable steps towards a journey to financial freedom. Join me in uncovering the trap of debt and embarking on a transformative journey towards a brighter financial future.

In today's society, debt has become a heavily normalized aspect of life. From credit card balances and student loans to mortgages and car payments, it seems like most people are living with some level of debt. However, what many fail to realize is that this constant state of owing money can be a trap that holds us back from achieving our dreams and living a fulfilling life.

As I delved deeper into the topic of debt, I found that there are various factors at play that contribute to its prevalence and hold over us. From societal pressures and consumerism to a lack of financial literacy and unforeseen circumstances, debt can sneak up on anyone and easily spiral out of control. But the good news is that it doesn't have to be this way.

Through my extensive research, I have identified key steps and strategies that can help individuals break free from the traps of debt and embark on a journey towards financial freedom. This book goes beyond the usual advice of cutting back on expenses and creating a budget, as it takes a holistic approach to addressing the root causes of debt and empowers readers to take control of their finances.

I have also included personal anecdotes from my own experience with debt, as well as insights from financial experts, to provide a well-rounded perspective and practical tips that readers can apply to their own situations. My goal with this book is to not only offer a solution to the trap of debt but also to inspire and motivate readers to take action towards a brighter financial future.

No matter where you are on your financial journey, whether you are struggling with debt or simply looking to improve your financial well-being, this book is for you. Join me on this transformative journey towards breaking free from debt and achieving financial empowerment. Let's uncover the trap of debt and take the first step towards a brighter financial future together.

Part I: Understanding the Cycle of Debt

Chapter 1: The Impact of Debt on Your Life and Well-Being

Debt is a growing problem in today's society, affecting individuals, families, and even entire countries. It is the state of owing money or something of value to someone else, usually in the form of a loan or credit card balance. While debt can sometimes be necessary for making large purchases, such as a car or home, it can quickly become a burden that impacts our lives and well-being in many ways.

The most obvious impact of debt is its financial strain. When we are in debt, we have less money available for our basic needs such as food, housing, and healthcare. This can lead to high levels of stress as we struggle to make ends meet and may result in having to sacrifice other important expenses, such as education or retirement savings.

Furthermore, being in debt can also negatively affect our credit score. This is a measure of our financial health that lenders use to determine our creditworthiness. A low credit score can make it difficult to get approved for loans, credit cards, or even a rental lease. It can also result in higher interest rates and fees, making it more challenging to pay off existing debts and leading to a never-ending cycle of debt.

Debt can also have a significant impact on our mental and emotional well-being. The constant worry and stress of being in debt can lead to anxiety, depression, and other mental health issues. We may feel ashamed or embarrassed about our financial situation, which can further damage our self-esteem and relationships.

Moreover, being in debt may prevent us from achieving our long-term goals and dreams. For example, we may have to postpone buying a house or starting a business due to our debt, significantly impacting our future financial stability and potential for growth.

In some cases, the impact of debt can also extend beyond the individual and have a broader effect on society. When a large portion of the population is burdened with debt, it can result in economic instability and slow down the overall growth of the economy.

In addition to the financial strain and impact on credit score, the stress of debt can also lead to physical health problems. Studies have shown that individuals in debt are more likely to experience headaches, migraines, and other physical symptoms associated with high levels of stress. They may also engage in unhealthy coping mechanisms, such as smoking, drinking, or overeating, to alleviate the stress of debt, which can further damage their physical well-being.

Furthermore, being in debt can also strain our relationships with friends and family. Constantly worrying about money and the inability to participate in social activities can create tension and lead to conflicts. Debt can also cause feelings of shame and guilt, causing individuals to isolate themselves from loved ones and further impacting their mental and emotional health.

Moreover, debt can also limit our career options and job opportunities. Employers may conduct credit checks as part of the hiring process, and a high level of debt can be seen as a red flag, affecting our chances of getting a job or a promotion. This can result in reduced job satisfaction and lower income, making it even more challenging to pay off debts.

Lastly, the impact of debt can create a sense of powerlessness and diminish our sense of control over our lives. This feeling of being overwhelmed and unable to change our financial situation can lead to a lack of motivation and a feeling of being stuck in a never-ending cycle of debt.

Overall, the impact of debt on our lives and well-being is far-reaching and multifaceted. It not only affects our financial stability but also our mental, emotional, and physical health, as well as our relationships and career opportunities. Understanding these effects can help us break free from the cycle of debt and take control of our financial future.

Chapter 2: The Psychology of Debt and How It Keeps Us Trapped

While debt undoubtedly has a significant impact on our lives and well-being, the cycle of debt is often perpetuated by psychological factors as well. The fear of missing out or keeping up with societal expectations can lead us to make impulsive and unnecessary purchases, putting us in debt.

Moreover, the convenience and ease of access to credit encourage us to spend beyond our means. With credit cards and loans readily available, it can be tempting to buy things we cannot afford at the moment without considering the long-term consequences. This leads to a sense of instant gratification, which can become addictive.

Additionally, debt can also trigger feelings of inadequacy and unworthiness. Society often associates success and happiness with material possessions and a certain lifestyle, leading us to believe that we need to spend more money to achieve these things. This mindset can lead to overspending and accumulating debt, reinforcing the cycle.

Furthermore, the constant pressure to maintain a certain standard of living can also lead to lifestyle inflation, where we increase our spending to match our income level. This can result in never-ending debt as our expenses keep rising with our income, making it challenging to break free from the cycle.

The emotional and psychological impact of debt can also lead to a sense of hopelessness and helplessness. As we struggle to make payments and see our debt balance constantly growing, we may feel trapped and believe that there is no way out.

The cycle of debt is a complex pattern that impacts our financial, mental, and emotional well-being. Breaking free from this cycle requires a deep understanding of the psychological factors that keep us trapped in debt and taking proactive steps towards improving our financial habits. Only by recognizing the impact of debt on our lives and addressing the root causes can we break free from this cycle and achieve financial stability and well-being. It is crucial to develop a healthy relationship with money and reframe our mindset surrounding debt. Instead of using debt to finance our wants and desires, we should focus on using it as a tool to achieve our long-term goals and financial stability.

It is also essential to learn how to manage our finances effectively and create a budget plan that aligns with our income and expenses. Making a conscious effort to track our spending, prioritize our needs over our wants, and save for the future can also help break the cycle of debt.

Additionally, seeking support from financial counselors, therapists, and support groups can also be beneficial in addressing the psychological factors that contribute to the cycle of debt. The key is to be proactive and take control of our finances to overcome the negative impacts of debt on our lives and well-being.

In the end, it is essential to remember that breaking free from the cycle of debt is a process that requires patience, determination, and a willingness to change our mindset and habits. By understanding the underlying psychological factors and taking positive steps, we can achieve financial freedom and improve our overall well-being.

One of the biggest challenges in breaking the cycle of debt is the societal stigma and shame attached to being in debt. Our culture often associates debt with failure and irresponsibility, leading people to feel embarrassed and avoid seeking help or even acknowledging their debt. This can further perpetuate the cycle as individuals may be unwilling to confront their debt and take necessary actions to address it.

Moreover, the constant bombardment of advertisements and social media showcasing a luxurious and materialistic lifestyle can also contribute to the cycle of debt. We are constantly exposed to images of people living the high life, which can create a sense of envy and a desire to attain the same status. As a result, we may be more likely to overspend and use debt to finance our wants rather than our needs.

The cycle of debt can also have detrimental effects on our mental and emotional health. Constantly worrying about debt and struggling to make payments can lead to stress, anxiety, and even depression. These mental health issues can further perpetuate the cycle of debt, as individuals may turn to overspending or using credit to cope with their emotions.

Moreover, being in debt can also impact our relationships, causing stress and conflicts with our partners, family, and friends. The financial strain of debt can strain relationships, leading to feelings of isolation and a lack of support.

To break free from the cycle of debt, it is important to address these psychological and emotional factors as well. Seeking professional help and support groups can provide a safe space to talk about our debt and the emotions surrounding it. It is essential to remember that being in debt does not make us a failure or a bad person, and seeking help is a brave and proactive step towards improving our financial well-being.

In conclusion, understanding the psychological factors that contribute to the cycle of debt is crucial to breaking free from it. By recognizing and addressing these factors, we can develop healthy financial habits, improve our relationships, and prioritize our overall well-being. Breaking the cycle of debt is a journey that requires self-reflection, patience, and persistence, but with determination and support, it is possible to achieve financial freedom and a healthier relationship with money.

Part II: Strategies for Breaking the Cycle of Debt
Chapter 3: Assessing Your Financial Situation: The First Step Towards Change

Breaking the cycle of debt can be a daunting and overwhelming task. It requires discipline, dedication, and a willingness to make difficult changes in your financial habits. The first and most crucial step in this journey is to assess your current financial situation. This step will serve as the foundation for creating a sustainable plan to break the cycle of debt.

In this chapter, we will explore the different strategies for assessing your financial situation and gaining a comprehensive understanding of your debt. By the end of this chapter, you will have a clear picture of your financial health, and you can move forward with confidence in creating a plan to break the cycle of debt.

1. Gather All Your Financial Information

The first step in assessing your financial situation is to gather all your financial information. This includes your bank statements, credit card bills, loan statements, and any other financial documents. It is essential to have a complete overview of your income, expenses, and debts before making any changes to your financial habits.

2. Calculate Your Debt-to-Income Ratio

Your debt-to-income ratio (DTI) is a crucial factor in understanding your financial situation. It is the percentage of your monthly income that goes towards paying off debts. To calculate your DTI, add up all your monthly debt payments and divide it by your monthly income. For example, if your total monthly debt payments are $2,000 and your monthly income is $5,000, your DTI is 40%.

A high DTI indicates that you are using a significant portion of your income to pay off debts, leaving you with less money for other essential expenses. Ideally, your DTI should be below 36%. If your DTI is higher, it is a sign that you need to take immediate action to begin reducing your debts.

3. Identify Your Debts

Make a list of all your debts, including credit cards, loans, and any other outstanding payments. Write down the total balance, minimum monthly payment, interest rate, and due date for each debt. This will help you understand the magnitude of your debts and prioritize which ones to pay off first.

4. Review Your Credit Report

Your credit report is a comprehensive record of all your credit accounts, loans, and payment history. It is essential to review your credit report regularly to check for any errors, inaccuracies, or fraudulent activity. These factors can significantly impact your credit score and hinder your ability to break the cycle of debt.

5. Analyze Your Expenses

Tracking and analyzing your expenses is a vital step in understanding your spending habits. Start by creating a budget and categorizing your expenses into essential and non-essential items. This will help you identify areas where you can cut back and save money. For example, you can reduce your monthly grocery expenses, limit eating out, or cancel unnecessary subscriptions.

6. Evaluate Your Income

Assess your income sources and determine if they are enough to cover your expenses and debts. If your income is not sufficient, consider finding alternative sources of income, such as a part-time job or freelance work. You may also need to negotiate a raise or promotion with your current employer to increase your income.

7. Seek Professional Assistance

If you are struggling to assess your financial situation or feel overwhelmed by the amount of debt, consider seeking professional help. A financial advisor or credit counselor can provide expert guidance and help you create an effective plan to break the cycle of debt.

Remember, the key to breaking the cycle of debt is to have a clear understanding of your financial situation. By following these strategies, you can gain valuable insights into your income, expenses, and debts and make informed decisions to begin your journey towards financial freedom.

Chapter 4: Budgeting: The Key to Regaining Control of Your Finances

Budgeting is a crucial tool for breaking the cycle of debt and regaining control over one's finances. It is the process of creating a plan for how to spend and save money based on an individual's income and expenses. Budgeting is not only about limiting one's spending; it also involves setting financial goals, tracking expenses, and making informed decisions about how and where to allocate funds. By creating and adhering to a budget, individuals can develop healthy financial habits and achieve long-term financial stability.

In this chapter, we will explore the importance of budgeting in breaking the cycle of debt and provide practical strategies for creating and sticking to a budget.

1. Understand your income and expenses: The first step in creating a budget is to understand your income and expenses. This includes all sources of income, such as salary, bonuses, and investments, as well as fixed expenses like rent, utilities, and loan payments, and variable expenses like groceries, entertainment, and transportation. It is essential to have a clear understanding of how much money is coming in and going out each month.

2. Categorize expenses: Once you have a comprehensive list of your income and expenses, categorize them into needs and wants. Needs are essential expenses that are crucial for survival, such as food, shelter, and transportation. Wants are non-essential expenses, such as dining out, entertainment, and luxury items. This categorization can help identify areas where you can cut back on spending and prioritize necessary expenses.

3. Set financial goals: Setting financial goals is an essential part of budgeting as it provides a sense of direction and motivates individuals to stick to their budget. These goals can be short-term, such as paying off credit card debt, or long-term, such as saving for retirement. Having a

clear understanding of your financial goals can help determine how much you need to save each month and which expenses you can adjust to reach those goals.

4. Track your expenses: Keeping track of expenses is crucial in budgeting as it allows you to see where your money is going and identify areas for improvement. There are various methods to track expenses, such as using a budgeting app, a spreadsheet, or pen and paper. Choose a method that works for you, and make it a habit to record all your expenses.

5. Identify areas for adjustment: Once you have a clear understanding of your income, expenses, and financial goals, it's time to identify areas where you can adjust your spending. This could include cutting back on discretionary expenses, negotiating for lower utility or insurance rates, or finding ways to increase your income. By making adjustments, you can free up more money to pay off debt or save for your financial goals.

6. Set realistic limits and stick to them: When creating a budget, it is crucial to set realistic limits for each expense category based on your income and financial goals. It's essential to be honest with yourself and not set unrealistic limits that you know you won't be able to stick to. Allow yourself some flexibility, but also hold yourself accountable for staying within the budget limits.

7. Plan for unexpected expenses: Inevitable financial emergencies like car repairs or medical bills can quickly derail a budget. To prevent this, it is essential to set aside money each month for unexpected expenses. This can help alleviate the financial burden when these types of emergencies arise.

8. Review and adjust your budget regularly: A budget is not a static document, and it should be reviewed regularly to ensure that it is still aligned with your financial goals and situation. It's essential to reassess and adjust your budget as needed to make sure it remains effective and realistic.

In conclusion, budgeting is a powerful tool for breaking the cycle of debt and regaining control over one's finances. By understanding your income and expenses, setting financial goals, tracking expenses, and making informed decisions, you can develop healthy financial habits and achieve long-term financial stability. It may require discipline and sacrifice in the short term, but the long-term benefits of budgeting far outweigh the temporary discomfort. Remember, a budget is a tool that helps you take control of your finances and make informed choices about how to spend and save your money.

Chapter 5: Tackling Debt: The Power of Debt Repayment Strategies

Debt is a burden that can weigh heavily on a person's finances and overall well-being. It is a cycle that can be difficult to break, but with the right strategies, it is possible to overcome it. In this chapter, we will discuss various effective strategies for breaking the cycle of debt and regaining financial stability.

1. Build a Budget: The first step towards tackling debt is to create a budget. This will help you understand your income and expenses and identify areas where you can cut back on spending. Make sure to prioritize your debt repayments in your budget and allocate a certain amount towards it each month.

2. Snowball or Avalanche Method: These are two popular strategies for debt repayment. The snowball method involves paying off the smallest debt first and then rolling over the payments into the next smallest debt and so on. This can provide a sense of accomplishment and motivation to continue paying off larger debts. The avalanche method, on the other hand, focuses on paying off debts with the highest interest rates first, saving you money on interest in the long run.

3. Debt Consolidation: Debt consolidation involves combining multiple debts into one single debt with a lower interest rate. This can decrease the overall amount you owe and make it easier to manage. It is important to carefully consider the terms and interest rates of the consolidation loan to ensure it is a beneficial option for your situation.

4. Negotiate with Creditors: If you are struggling to make payments, consider negotiating with your creditors. They may be willing to lower your interest rate, reduce your payments, or even settle for a lower amount. It is important to communicate with them and explain your financial situation to find a feasible solution.

5. Seek Professional Help: If you are overwhelmed with debt, it may be beneficial to seek help from a credit counseling agency or a financial advisor. They can help you create a debt management plan, negotiate with creditors, and provide you with valuable financial advice.

6. Increase your Income: One way to tackle debt is by increasing your income. Consider taking on a part-time job or freelancing to bring in extra money that can be used towards your debt repayments. You can also ask for a raise at your current job or look for better job opportunities.

7. Cut Expenses: Along with increasing your income, it is equally important to cut down on unnecessary expenses. Look for ways to save on your monthly bills, reduce eating out, and avoid unnecessary purchases. Every penny saved can be put towards your debt repayment.

8. Avoid Taking on New Debt: While working towards paying off your existing debt, it is important to avoid taking on any new debt. This means avoiding unnecessary credit card purchases and high-interest loans. Focus on paying off your current debts before taking on any new financial obligations.

9. Seek Financial Education: Often, people get into debt because of a lack of financial education. Consider taking a financial literacy course or reading books on personal finance to learn about managing your money effectively. This will help you avoid future debt and make informed financial decisions.

10. Stay Focused and Motivated: Tackling debt can be a long and challenging process, but it is crucial to stay focused and motivated. Keep track of your progress and celebrate small victories. Remember your ultimate goal of becoming debt-free and use it as motivation to continue working towards it.

Breaking the cycle of debt requires persistence, determination, and a solid plan of action. By implementing these strategies, you can take control of your finances and overcome the burden of debt. Remember, it takes time and effort, but with patience and discipline, you can achieve financial freedom and live a debt-free life.

Chapter 6: Increasing Your Income: Finding Ways to Make More Money

Debt can be a vicious cycle that is hard to break out of. Many people find themselves in a never-ending cycle of borrowing money to pay off previous debts, leading to a constant increase in their overall debt load. This can be incredibly stressful and overwhelming, and it often feels like there is no way out. However, there are strategies that can be employed to break the cycle of debt, and one of the most effective ways is to increase one's income.

In this chapter, we will explore various strategies for increasing one's income and finding ways to make more money. These strategies can help individuals pay off their debts faster and get out of the cycle of debt for good.

1. Look for a Higher-Paying Job: The most obvious and straightforward way to increase your income is to get a higher-paying job. This may involve brushing up on your skills, updating your resume, and actively searching for better-paying opportunities. Consider exploring new industries or taking on a more challenging role that offers a higher salary. It may also be worth negotiating for a raise at your current job, especially if you have been there for a while and have a good track record.

2. Take on a Side Hustle: In today's gig economy, there are countless opportunities to earn extra income through side jobs or freelance work. This could be anything from driving for a ridesharing service to selling handmade goods on Etsy. Look for opportunities that align with your skills, interests, and schedule. This extra income can go a long way toward paying off debt and breaking the cycle of borrowing.

3. Monetize Your Hobbies and Talents: Do you have a talent or hobby that you are passionate about? Consider monetizing it. You could offer private music lessons, sell handmade crafts, or start a blog or YouTube channel.

With the right marketing and determination, these hobbies can quickly turn into a profitable side business.

4. Rent Out Your Space: If you have an extra room in your home or a vacation property, consider renting it out on platforms like Airbnb. This can be a great way to earn some extra income without committing to a part-time job. Just be sure to do your research and set appropriate prices to ensure you are making a profit.

5. Invest in Yourself: Investing in yourself can also lead to increased income. This could involve taking courses to improve your skills or pursuing a higher degree. These investments in yourself can make you more competitive in the job market, which can lead to higher-paying opportunities.

6. Negotiate for Better Pay: When starting a new job, don't be afraid to negotiate for better pay or benefits. Many people settle for lower salaries because they are afraid to ask for more. But by doing your research on typical salaries in your industry and being confident in your skills and experience, you may be able to negotiate a better salary and increase your income.

7. Leverage Your Network: Your personal and professional networks can also be a valuable resource for finding ways to make more money. Reach out to friends, family, and colleagues to see if they know of any job opportunities or if they can refer you to someone in their network. You never know where a simple conversation can lead.

8. Start a Business: If you have an entrepreneurial spirit, starting your own business can be an excellent way to increase your income. This can be anything from a small side hustle to a full-time venture. With careful planning and hard work, your business can grow and provide you with a stable source of income.

In conclusion, increasing your income is a crucial step in breaking the cycle of debt. By implementing these strategies and being proactive in finding ways to make more money, you can increase your income and pay off your debt faster. It may require some sacrifice and hard work, but the long-term benefits of breaking the cycle of debt and achieving financial freedom are worth the effort. Remember to stay disciplined and focused on your goal, and you will be on your way to a debt-free future.

Chapter 7: Saving and Investing: Building a Strong Financial Future

In today's consumer-driven society, it can be easy to fall into the cycle of debt. With easy access to credit cards, loans, and other forms of financing, many people find themselves struggling to keep up with their monthly payments and sinking deeper and deeper into debt. The good news is that it is possible to break this cycle and build a strong financial future. This chapter will discuss some strategies for saving and investing to help individuals break the cycle of debt and achieve financial stability.

1. Create a Budget and Stick to It

The first step in breaking the cycle of debt is to create a budget. This involves identifying your income and expenses and then setting limits on your spending. It's important to be realistic when creating your budget and to include all of your monthly expenses, such as rent or mortgage, bills, groceries, and any debt payments. Once you have a budget in place, it's important to stick to it. This will help you avoid overspending, ensure that you have enough money to cover your monthly expenses, and make progress towards paying off any debt.

2. Minimize Unnecessary Expenses

To break the cycle of debt, it's important to minimize unnecessary expenses. This means taking a hard look at your spending habits and identifying areas where you can cut back. This could include things like eating out, buying expensive coffees, or subscribing to unnecessary services. By reducing these expenses, you can free up more money to put towards savings and paying off debt.

3. Build an Emergency Fund

One of the main reasons people fall into debt is because they do not have savings to cover unexpected expenses. To avoid this, it's important to build an emergency fund. This should be a separate savings account that you can tap into when an unexpected expense arises, such as a car repair or medical bill. Ideally, your emergency fund should be able to cover at least three to six months' worth of expenses. This will provide a safety net and help you avoid taking on more debt in the future.

4. Focus on Paying Off Debt

If you are in debt, it's important to make it a priority to pay it off. This may mean cutting back on unnecessary expenses or finding ways to increase your income. One effective strategy for paying off debt is the debt snowball method, where you focus on paying off your smallest debt first and then use the money you were putting towards it to pay off your next smallest debt, and so on. This approach can help you build momentum and make progress towards paying off all of your debts.

5. Consider Debt Consolidation

Debt consolidation involves combining multiple debts into one loan with a lower interest rate. This can make it easier to manage your debt and may even help you save money on interest payments. However, it's important to carefully consider the terms and conditions of the consolidation loan and make sure that it is the right choice for your financial situation.

6. Save for Retirement

While it may seem counterintuitive to save for retirement when you are in debt, it's still important to do so. Putting money towards your retirement savings, such as a 401(k) or IRA, can help you build a strong financial future and be better prepared for unexpected expenses.

7. Educate Yourself About Investing

Investing is an important tool for building wealth and achieving financial stability. It's important to educate yourself about the basics of investing and develop a long-term investment strategy. This could involve working with a financial advisor or doing your own research to find the best investment options for you.

Conclusion:

Breaking the cycle of debt and achieving financial stability is not an easy task, but with the right strategies, it is possible. By creating a budget, minimizing unnecessary expenses, building an emergency fund, focusing on paying off debt, considering debt consolidation, saving for retirement, and educating yourself about investing, you can break the cycle of debt and build a strong financial future. It will require discipline and commitment, but the rewards of financial stability and freedom are well worth the effort. So start implementing these strategies today and take control of your finances for a better tomorrow.

Part III: Beyond Debt: Building Wealth and Financial Security

Chapter 8: Smart Credit Management: How to Use Credit to Your Advantage

In the previous chapters, we have discussed the importance of managing debt and understanding its impact on our financial health. But beyond debt, there is another crucial aspect of personal finance that often gets overlooked – building wealth and financial security.

Having a positive credit history and strong financial standing can open up countless opportunities for individuals and families to achieve their long-term financial goals. In this chapter, we will delve into the world of credit and how it can be used to your advantage in building wealth and financial security.

Understanding Credit and its Importance

First and foremost, it is essential to understand what credit means and its role in our financial lives. Credit refers to the ability to borrow money or access goods and services with the promise of paying it back at a later date, usually with interest. It is a vital tool that allows individuals and businesses to make significant purchases, such as buying a house or starting a business, that they may not be able to afford in one lump sum.

Having good credit can bring many benefits. It can help in obtaining loans at lower interest rates, qualifying for better credit card rewards, and even landing a job, as some employers do a credit check as part of their hiring process. On the other hand, a poor credit history can lead to high interest rates, difficulty getting approved for loans, and limited financial options.

Therefore, it is crucial to understand how to manage credit wisely and use it to your advantage.

Building and Maintaining Good Credit

The foundation for using credit to your advantage lies in building and maintaining a good credit score. A credit score is a three-digit number that represents an individual's creditworthiness, and it is based on their credit history. The higher the credit score, the more creditworthy a person is considered.

To build a good credit score, four factors play a significant role – payment history, credit utilization ratio, credit mix, and length of credit history.

Payment history refers to how consistently a person makes on-time payments on their credit accounts. It accounts for about 35% of the credit score, making it the most crucial factor. It is vital to pay all credit card bills and loan payments on time to maintain a good payment history.

The credit utilization ratio is the percentage of credit being used compared to the total credit available. It accounts for about 30% of the credit score, and it is recommended to keep it below 30%. A higher credit utilization ratio can indicate a higher risk of defaulting on payments.

Credit mix refers to the various types of credit accounts an individual has, such as credit cards, mortgages, car loans, and student loans. It accounts for about 10% of the credit score, and having a diverse mix of credit shows responsible credit management.

Lastly, the length of credit history looks at how long a person has had credit accounts open. It accounts for about 15% of the credit score, and a longer credit history typically reflects a higher level of creditworthiness.

Tips for Smart Credit Management

Here are some tips to help you use credit to your advantage and build a solid credit history:

1. Make payments on time: As mentioned earlier, your payment history accounts for a significant portion of your credit score. Be sure to pay all your credit accounts on time, even if it is just the minimum payment.

2. Keep credit balances low: A high credit utilization ratio can negatively impact your credit score. Aim to keep your credit card balances below 30% of the credit limit.

3. Monitor your credit report: Regularly check your credit report to ensure that all information is accurate and to catch any potential errors or fraudulent activities.

4. Limit new credit applications: Every time you apply for new credit, it results in a hard inquiry on your credit report, which can lower your credit score. Only apply for credit when necessary, and try to space out applications to minimize the impact on your score.

5. Diversify your credit mix: As mentioned earlier, having different types of credit accounts can improve your credit score. Consider adding a credit card or small loan to your credit mix if you only have one type of credit account.

6. Avoid closing old credit accounts: The length of your credit history is an essential factor in your credit score. If you need to close a credit account, try to keep the oldest one open to maintain a longer credit history.

Using Credit to Build Wealth and Financial Security

Now that you understand how to build and maintain good credit, let's explore how it can help you build wealth and financial security.

1. Lower interest rates: With a good credit score, you are more likely to qualify for lower interest rates on loans, such as mortgages and car loans. This can save you thousands of dollars in interest payments over the life of the loan.

2. Access to credit: Having good credit means you have the option to borrow money if needed. This can be useful in times of emergencies or when making significant purchases that can help you build wealth in the long run, such as investing in a business.

3. Better credit card rewards: Credit card companies often offer more generous rewards and perks to individuals with good credit scores. This can include cashback, travel points, or discounts, which can save you money and contribute to your overall financial security.

4. Rental opportunities: Many landlords and property management companies require a credit check before renting out their properties. With a good credit history, you are more likely to qualify for a desirable rental property, which can save you money on rent and improve your living situation.

Conclusion

In short, credit can be a valuable tool for building wealth and achieving financial security. By understanding how to manage credit wisely, maintaining a solid credit history, and utilizing credit to your advantage, you can open up doors to a more financially stable and secure future. Remember, good credit takes time to build, so start early and make smart credit management a priority in your financial journey.

Chapter 9: Creating a Sustainable Financial Plan: Setting Goals and Achieving Them

Creating a sustainable financial plan is essential for building wealth and achieving long-term financial security. It requires setting clear goals and developing a roadmap to achieve them. In this chapter, we will explore the key elements of a sustainable financial plan and how to set realistic goals that can be successfully achieved.

1. Define Your Financial Goals
The first step in creating a sustainable financial plan is to define your financial goals. These goals will serve as the foundation for all your financial decisions and actions. It is important to have both short-term and long-term goals, as well as specific and measurable objectives.

Short-term goals typically involve immediate financial needs, such as paying off debt, saving for a down payment on a house, or building an emergency fund. Long-term goals, on the other hand, require more strategic planning and can include saving for retirement, investing in your children's education, or starting a business.

2. Prioritize Your Goals
Once you have identified your financial goals, it is important to prioritize them. This will help you determine which goals are most important and which ones can be put on hold. It is crucial to be realistic and prioritize your goals based on your current financial situation.

For example, if you have a lot of debt, your priority should be to pay it off before focusing on other goals. Or if you have young children, saving for their education might be a higher priority than saving for retirement. Prioritizing your goals will help you make informed decisions and stay on track with your financial plan.

3. Create a Realistic Timeline
Having a timeline for your financial goals is crucial for creating a sustainable financial plan. It helps you stay accountable and on track with

your progress. When setting a timeline, make sure it is both realistic and flexible. This means considering factors such as your income, expenses, and any potential changes in your life that may affect your goals.

For example, if your goal is to save for a down payment on a house, make sure to factor in how much you can save each month and how long it will take to reach your target amount. If your timeline is too short, you may end up compromising on other financial priorities or taking on too much debt to meet your goal. On the other hand, a timeline that is too long may result in losing momentum and taking longer to achieve your goals.

4. Set Actionable Steps

Once you have identified your goals and established a timeline, the next crucial step is to break them down into actionable steps. This means identifying the specific actions you need to take to achieve each goal. For example, if your goal is to save for retirement, your actionable steps could include opening a retirement account, contributing a certain amount each month, and investing in a diverse portfolio.

Breaking down your goals into smaller, actionable steps makes them more manageable and less overwhelming. It also allows you to track your progress and make adjustments along the way, if needed.

5. Continuously Monitor and Review Your Plan

Creating a sustainable financial plan is not a one-time process. It requires continuous monitoring and reviewing to ensure you stay on track and make necessary adjustments. Life is unpredictable, and your financial goals may change over time. Therefore, it is essential to regularly review your plan and make necessary adjustments to keep it aligned with your current goals and financial situation.

It is also important to regularly track your progress and celebrate your achievements. This will help keep you motivated and focused on achieving your goals.

In conclusion, creating a sustainable financial plan is key to building wealth and achieving long-term financial security. It involves defining your financial goals, prioritizing them, setting a realistic timeline, breaking them down into actionable steps, and regularly monitoring and reviewing your plan. With a well-crafted financial plan, you can achieve your goals and create a strong financial foundation for yourself and your family.

Chapter 10: Building Wealth: Strategies for Wealth Accumulation and Protection

In the previous two chapters, we discussed the importance of managing debt and setting a strong financial foundation. However, simply managing debt and having a stable financial situation is not enough to secure long-term financial success. In order to truly build wealth and achieve financial security, it is crucial to have a plan for wealth accumulation and protection. In this chapter, we will explore the key strategies and principles for building wealth and protecting it for the future.

1. Set financial goals and create a plan

The first step towards building wealth is to have a clear understanding of your financial goals. This could include paying off debt, saving for retirement, buying a house, starting a business, or a combination of these. Once you have identified your goals, it is important to create a comprehensive financial plan that outlines how you will achieve them.

Your plan should include specific, measurable, achievable, relevant, and time-bound (SMART) goals. This will help you stay on track and monitor your progress. Your plan should also consider factors such as your current income, expenses, and risk tolerance. It should be reviewed and adjusted regularly, as your financial situation and goals may change over time.

2. Invest wisely

One of the key strategies for wealth accumulation is investing wisely. Investing allows you to grow your money beyond what you can earn through a savings account or other low-risk options. However, it is important to understand that investing involves taking on some level of risk.

Diversification is a crucial aspect of smart investing. This means spreading your investments across different asset classes, such as stocks, bonds, real estate, and cash, to reduce the overall risk of your portfolio. It is also important to regularly review and rebalance your investments to ensure they align with your risk tolerance and financial goals.

3. Take advantage of retirement accounts and employer benefits

Retirement planning is a crucial component of building long-term wealth. Take advantage of retirement accounts such as a 401(k) or Individual Retirement Account (IRA) to save for your future. These accounts offer tax benefits, compound interest, and potential employer contributions, making them a powerful tool for wealth accumulation.

Additionally, be sure to understand and take advantage of any employer benefits, such as a matching contribution to your retirement account, health insurance, or employee stock purchase plans. These benefits can significantly increase your wealth-building potential.

4. Avoid lifestyle inflation

As your income grows, it can be tempting to increase your spending and lifestyle accordingly. However, this can hinder your wealth-building goals. Instead, strive to keep your expenses in check and avoid unnecessary debt or lifestyle inflation. This will free up more money to save and invest, accelerating your wealth-building journey.

5. Create multiple streams of income

Having multiple streams of income can provide you with security and flexibility in times of economic uncertainty. Consider exploring different sources of income, such as starting a side hustle, investing in rental properties, or earning passive income through dividends or rental income. However, it is important to research and carefully manage the risks associated with each stream of income.

6. Protect your wealth through insurance

Protecting your wealth is just as important as building it. This includes having proper insurance coverage to protect your assets and income in the event of unexpected events such as a job loss, disability, or natural disaster.

Consider purchasing health, life, disability, and homeowner's or renter's insurance. These policies can provide a safety net and prevent a financial setback in case of an emergency.

7. Plan for taxes and estate planning

Tax planning and estate planning are essential components of protecting your wealth. Proper tax planning can help minimize your tax burden and increase your after-tax income, allowing you to save and invest more. Additionally, having a comprehensive estate plan in place can ensure that your assets are distributed according to your wishes and avoid costly legal battles.

In conclusion, building wealth and achieving financial security requires discipline, patience, and a comprehensive plan. By following these key strategies and principles, you can create a strong financial foundation and work towards achieving your long-term financial goals. Remember, wealth building is a marathon, not a sprint, and requires consistent effort and dedication. Stay focused on your goals and make adjustments as needed to ensure your financial success.

Chapter 11: Teaching the Next Generation: Passing on Financial Knowledge and Values

In the quest for financial well-being and security, one of the crucial aspects often overlooked is the importance of passing on financial knowledge and values to the next generation. Part III of "Beyond Debt: Building Wealth and Financial Security" delves into Chapter 11, which focuses on the significance of teaching the younger generation about managing money, investing wisely, and cultivating positive financial habits.

The Importance of Financial Education for the Next Generation

Financial literacy is an invaluable skill that empowers individuals to make informed decisions about their money. In Chapter 11, the emphasis is on the younger generation, acknowledging that instilling financial knowledge early can have a lasting impact. This section explores why teaching the next generation about finances is crucial for their long-term well-being and how it contributes to the overall financial health of society.

1. Early Exposure to Financial Concepts

The chapter begins by discussing the importance of early exposure to financial concepts. Introducing children to basic financial principles at an age-appropriate level lays the foundation for a lifetime of responsible money management. From understanding the concept of saving to grasping the basics of budgeting, the goal is to provide a gradual and age-appropriate introduction to financial matters.

2. The Role of Schools and Educational Institutions

Recognizing that not all children receive financial education at home, the chapter explores the role of schools and educational institutions in filling this gap. It discusses the integration of financial literacy into school curricula, promoting the idea that financial education should be a fundamental component of a well-rounded education.

3. Teaching Practical Skills: Budgeting, Saving, and Investing

Moving beyond theoretical knowledge, the chapter delves into practical skills. It provides insights into how parents, guardians, and educators can teach children the hands-on skills of budgeting, saving, and investing. The focus is on making financial education relatable and engaging, using real-life examples and age-appropriate activities.

Strategies for Teaching Financial Literacy

The chapter doesn't just highlight the importance of financial education; it also provides actionable strategies for effectively teaching financial literacy to the next generation.

1. Interactive Learning Approaches

Understanding that traditional teaching methods may not capture the attention of young minds, the chapter advocates for interactive learning approaches. It explores the use of games, simulations, and other interactive tools to make financial education enjoyable and memorable.

2. Leading by Example: Parental and Mentor Influence

An essential aspect of passing on financial values is the influence of parents, guardians, and mentors. The chapter explores how leading by example can significantly impact a child's financial mindset. It discusses ways in which adults can model responsible financial behavior and foster a positive attitude toward money.

3. Addressing the Emotional Aspect of Money

Beyond the practical aspects of financial education, the chapter delves into the emotional aspect of money. It explores how discussions about values, attitudes toward wealth, and understanding the emotional connection to money play a pivotal role in shaping a child's financial identity.

Cultivating Financial Values

The final section delves into the importance of instilling positive financial values. It explores the role of ethics, responsibility, and social consciousness in financial decision-making. By emphasizing the connection between financial success and social responsibility, the chapter encourages the cultivation of values that contribute to both personal and societal well-being.

Conclusion

Chapter 11 serves as a comprehensive guide on how to teach the next generation about financial matters, emphasizing the long-term impact of early financial education. By providing practical strategies, emphasizing interactive learning, and exploring the influence of parental and mentorship roles, this chapter aims to equip readers with the tools to shape financially responsible and ethically aware individuals. In doing so, it contributes not only to the financial well-being of individuals but also to the broader economic health and stability of society.

Conclusion:
Breaking the Cycle and Living a Life of Financial Freedom

In life, we often find ourselves caught in a cycle – whether it is a pattern of behavior, a routine, or even a mindset. One of the most common and difficult cycles to break is that of financial struggle. Many individuals and families find themselves constantly living paycheck to paycheck, drowning in debt, and struggling to make ends meet. However, breaking this cycle and achieving financial freedom is not impossible. With the right mindset and actions, anyone can turn their financial situation around and live a life of financial freedom.

The first step towards breaking the cycle of financial struggle is to acknowledge the root causes. This may be overspending, living beyond means, or not having a budget in place. It is important to identify the areas that hold you back financially and work towards addressing them. The most crucial aspect of this step is to take responsibility for your financial situation. Blaming external factors or circumstances will only perpetuate the cycle. By taking ownership and realizing that you have the power to change your financial fate, you are already on the path to financial freedom.

Next, it is essential to create a plan and set achievable goals. Without a plan, it is easy to fall back into old habits and continue the cycle of financial struggle. A budget is a useful tool to track income, expenses, and prioritize financial goals. It helps to identify unnecessary expenses and make necessary adjustments to increase savings and pay off debts. It is also crucial to set achievable goals, both short and long term. These goals will act as motivation and guide you in making sound financial decisions.

One of the most challenging parts of breaking the cycle of financial struggle is making sacrifices and being disciplined. It may mean cutting back on luxury items, downsizing, or taking in extra work. It requires discipline to stick to a budget, avoid unnecessary purchases, and stay consistent with financial goals. However, with each sacrifice and disciplined action, you are one step closer to financial freedom.

Creating multiple streams of income is another crucial step towards breaking the cycle of financial struggle. Many people rely only on their primary job for income, which can be risky. Having multiple sources of income, such as a side hustle or investments, not only increases income but also provides a safety net in case of unforeseen circumstances. This also allows for financial flexibility and the ability to save and invest for future financial stability.

Another important aspect of breaking the cycle of financial struggle is to surround yourself with the right people. The people we associate with have a significant impact on our mindset and financial habits. It is essential to surround yourself with individuals who have healthy financial habits and can support and motivate you on your journey towards financial freedom. This may include seeking out a financial advisor or joining a supportive community of like-minded individuals.

In conclusion, breaking the cycle of financial struggle and achieving financial freedom is not a quick fix but a journey that requires determination, discipline, and consistency. It is a mindset shift from living paycheck to paycheck to being in control of your financial destiny. By taking responsibility, creating a plan, making sacrifices, diversifying income, and surrounding yourself with the right people, anyone can break the cycle and live a life of financial freedom. It may not be easy, but the long-term benefits of financial stability and independence are worth the effort. So, start today, take charge of your finances, and break the cycle for good.

Debt-Tracking Spreadsheet for Easy Budgeting:

One of the first steps towards financial empowerment is taking control of your debts. A debt-tracking spreadsheet can help you keep track of all your debts, including credit card balances, loans, and other forms of debt. This tool allows you to see the bigger picture of your financial situation so you can create a plan to pay off your debts.

A debt-tracking spreadsheet typically includes columns for the creditor, interest rate, balance, minimum monthly payment, and due date. You can also add columns to track your payments and monitor your progress. This can help you prioritize which debts to pay off first based on interest rates or payment due dates.

By regularly updating your debt-tracking spreadsheet, you can see how your debts are decreasing over time. This can be a motivator to stick to your budget and make consistent payments. It also helps you identify any problem areas, such as high-interest debts or late payments, that may need to be addressed.

Recommended Reading: Must-Read Books for Financial Empowerment:

Reading books about personal finance and money management is a great way to learn about financial empowerment. There are a variety of books available on the market, catering to different levels of financial knowledge and goals. Some recommended reading includes:

1. "The Total Money Makeover" by Dave Ramsey: This popular book provides practical advice for getting out of debt and building wealth.

2. "Rich Dad Poor Dad" by Robert Kiyosaki: This book challenges traditional notions of wealth and teaches readers how to change their mindset to achieve financial success.

3. "The Millionaire Next Door" by Thomas J. Stanley and William D. Danko: This book dispels common myths about wealth and offers insights on how to become wealthy through responsible spending habits and investment strategies.

4. "I Will Teach You to Be Rich" by Ramit Sethi: This book provides a six-week plan for achieving financial success and creating a rich life.

5. "A Random Walk Down Wall Street" by Burton G. Malkiel: This book offers a comprehensive guide to investing and building wealth in the stock market.

Financial Planning Checklist for a Stronger Financial Future:

To achieve financial empowerment, it's important to have a plan in place. A financial planning checklist can help ensure that you are covering all the necessary steps to secure a stronger financial future. Here are some items that may be included in a financial planning checklist:

1. Set financial goals: Identify short-term and long-term financial goals that you want to achieve.

2. Create a budget: Determine your income and expenses to create a budget that aligns with your financial goals.

3. Review your credit report: Check your credit report for accuracy and address any errors.

4. Pay off high-interest debts: Prioritize paying off high-interest debts to save money on interest payments.

5. Start an emergency fund: Aim to save at least three to six months' worth of living expenses in case of unexpected financial emergencies.

6. Invest for retirement: Start planning for retirement early through employer-sponsored plans like 401(k)s or individual retirement accounts (IRAs).

7. Consider insurance: Make sure you and your family are protected with adequate insurance, such as health insurance, life insurance, and disability insurance.

8. Save for other goals: Consider saving for other goals, such as a down payment on a house, college tuition, or a dream vacation.

Tips for Saving and Investing on a Tight Budget:

Even if your budget is tight, there are still ways to save and invest for a stronger financial future. Here are some tips to help you save and invest on a tight budget:

1. Track your expenses: Take a closer look at where your money is going and identify areas where you can cut back.

2. Set up automatic savings and investments: Set up automatic transfers from your checking account to a savings account or investment account to ensure that you are consistently saving and investing.

3. Use apps and tools: There are many budgeting and savings apps available that can help you keep track of your expenses and save money.

4. Save any extra income: If you receive a raise or a bonus, consider putting that extra income towards your savings or investments.

5. Invest in low-cost options: Look for low-cost investment options, such as index funds, that can help you save on fees and expenses.

6. Take advantage of employer-sponsored plans: If your employer offers a 401(k) or similar retirement plan, try to contribute at least enough to get the maximum employer match.

7. Consider a side hustle: Consider taking on a side hustle or additional source of income to supplement your budget and save more.

8. Be patient: Building a strong financial future takes time and patience. Be consistent with your saving and investing habits, and over time, you will see the result of your efforts.

Remember, even small efforts to save and invest can make a big impact on your financial future. Be mindful of your spending, take advantage of savings opportunities, and stay committed to your financial goals. With time and patience, you can achieve financial stability and security, even on a tight budget.